# *Grief &* MOURNING

*When Someone or Something*
*You Love is No Longer There*

# Grief & MOURNING

*When Someone or Something
You Love is No Longer There*

# DAVE WILLIAMS

Unless otherwise indicated, all Scripture quotations are taken from the King James Version of the Bible.

## Grief and Mourning
When Someone Or Something You Love
Is No Longer There

*Copyright ©2001 by David R. Williams*

First Printing 2001

ISBN   0-93802-53-6

Published by

# DECAPOLIS
# PUBLISHING

Printed in the United States of America

MHC   10  9  8  7  6  5  4  3  2

# BOOKS BY DAVE WILLIAMS

*AIDS Plague*
*Beauty of Holiness*
*Christian Job Hunter's Handbook*
*Desires of Your Heart*
*Depression, Cave of Torment*
*Genuine Prosperity, The Power To Get Wealth*
*Getting To Know Your Heavenly Father*
*Gifts That Shape Your Life And Change Your World*
*Grand Finale Revival*
*Growing Up in Our Father's Family*
*How to Be a High Performance Believer
        in Low Octane Days*
*How You Can Be Filled With The Holy Spirit*
*Laying On of Hands*
*Lonely in the Midst of a Crowd*
*The New Life . . . The Start of Something Wonderful*
*La Nueva Vida (The New Life . . . SPANISH)*
*Pacesetting Leadership*
*The Pastor's Pay*
*Patient Determination*
*The Road To Radical Riches*
*Revival Power of Music*
*Remedy for Worry and Tension*
*Secret of Power With God*
*Seven Signposts on the Road to Spiritual Maturity*
*Slain in the Spirit — Real or Fake?*
*Somebody Out There Needs You*
*Success Principles From the Lips of Jesus*
*Supernatural Soulwinning*
*The Miracle Results of Fasting*
*Thirty-Six Minutes with the Pastor*
*Understanding Spiritual Gifts*
*What To Do If You Miss The Rapture*

*This book is dedicated to the memory of*
*"My little buddy with the fake tattoo,"*
*Gabrielle Christian Salem, who went to Heaven on*
*November 23, 1999.*

# Contents

Rebel Or Rebound?..................................... 11

How Grief Gets A Grip ................................ 15

Is Grieving Good For You?....................... 19

Symptoms Of The Spirit Of Grief .......... 25

The Road To Recovery ............................ 33

"*I know you want to go forward and not backward. You want to become better, not bitter. You want to rebound, not rebel.*"

CHAPTER ONE

# REBEL OR REBOUND?

As a pastor I have seen a great deal of grief and mourning over the years. I have noticed two very different outcomes in people's lives who have experienced a loss.

I have seen people rebound and I have seen people rebel. I was one who rebelled, so I have some first-hand experience at the tragedy of rebellion.

## *Why A Young Boy Rebelled*

I knew something was wrong. Mom always woke us for school by 7:00 a.m. But this chilly November morning in 1966 was different. My little brother and I woke up late and heard a commotion downstairs. "What's wrong?" we wondered. Then it happened. Mom came limping up the steps, weeping, and told us the news, "Kids, dad died at 3:00 in the morning. He's dead."

"No, no!" we both screamed. I ran into the bathroom and cried, "God, bring him back, bring him back." It seemed like a nightmare, but I couldn't wake up. I was only 15 years old and my brother was just 13. My mind went to all the times dad had taken us fishing, or played catch with us in the backyard. I thought about the weekly trips we would make to the dairy for ice cream cones. I couldn't even imagine how it would be without him. I felt lost — abandoned.

Soon, the preacher showed up at the house. He told us that God's ways are mysterious and that Heaven needed my dad more than we needed him. In essence, he told us that God had taken my dad from us for a reason and we should just accept this as a fact of life. He meant well, I'm sure, but for some reason I hated hearing his words. He tried to comfort us, but instead his words were tormenting.

"What kind of a God would kill a 40-year-old man, and take him from his loving wife and children?" I reasoned. Being raised in a "traditional" church, we were clueless concerning the true nature and character of God. And, thus, I rebelled. I quit church. I quit Sunday School, and at age 16, I started drinking alcohol and doing every wild and corrupt thing I could. I joined the Navy and became even wilder, not wanting to have anything to do with the God who killed my dad.

I did not realize that in my rebellion I was actually running *with* the god who killed my dad — the devil. I didn't realize it until I met some guys who understood the Bible — God's Word. After chatting with me for weeks, they finally led me to the authentic Christ and taught me about the wonderful love of the real God. I learned then that God did not "take" my dad. I learned that God is a good God and the devil is a bad devil. I had been deceived. I was rebelling against the God who had created me and whose wish it was that I prosper and be in health (3 John 2). If only I had known.

During those rebellious years, I suffered two serious car accidents, had permanent scars imprinted on my face, and picked up some dangerous and disgusting habits. How I wished I had not rebelled. If I had really known the God of the Bible, instead of the "god" that well-meaning, but misguided, preacher told me about, I could have rebounded and saved myself a mammoth amount of pain and suffering.

## *To Rebound Or Rebel*

This is what happens when a person suffers a loss or a perceived loss. They either rebel or they rebound. Those who don't know and trust in Jesus Christ and His Word usually rebel. Those who do know and trust Jesus Christ rebound and turn out prospering more than ever.

# CHAPTER TWO

# HOW GRIEF GETS A GRIP

## *Grief Gets A Grip Through A Loss*

In 1929 when the stock market crashed, many perceived a loss. Fortunes disintegrated overnight. Suicide rates skyrocketed. Even some of Wall Street's best-known names took their own lives in despair, grieving over their losses. Grief can turn to suicide.

I have an Associated Press article that appeared in the paper just after New Year's Day. A 22-year-old boy wrote a suicide note, climbed into his silver Mazda on New Year's Eve, sped up to 50 mph, and drove off a cliff, killing himself. He was grieving over his mother who had died a year and a half ago.

Hanging onto grief is like hanging onto a snake egg. It may feel warm, but eventually that egg will hatch, and you won't like the results. One of the devil's lures is the lure of grief. He uses it to keep people from fulfilling God's purposes in their lives.

> They hatch cockatrice eggs, and weave the spider's web: he that eateth of their eggs dieth, and that which is crushed breaketh out into a viper.

> — Isaiah 59:5

## Mourning And Grief Are Not The Same

Grief is not the same as mourning. Grief is something that can drill deep into the heart of a person and can actually change the human personality, creating monstrous and abhorrent behavior. Mourning is simply an outward expression of an inward pain. Mourning will turn to dancing.

> Thou hast turned for me my mourning into dancing; thou hast put off my sackcloth, and girded me with gladness.

> — Psalm:30:11

Mourning and sorrow will flee away ... unless a person who is mourning picks up the spirit of grief, which will lead to further loss and eventual destruction.

> ...They shall obtain gladness and joy; and sorrow and mourning shall flee away.
>
> — Isaiah 51:11c

Someone may try to correct me by quoting the Scriptures about Jesus grieving, and the Holy Spirit grieving (Mark 3:5; Ephesians 4:30). Yet we need to understand that there are different Greek and Hebrew words for "grief." Jesus was grieved over the hardness of people's hearts. The Holy Spirit gets grieved over disobedience in the life of the believer. Paul was grieved in his spirit over a demon-possessed girl's words and actions (Acts 16:18), and we are told that Daniel was grieved in his spirit (Daniel 7:15). I am not talking about *that* kind of grief. I am talking about relentless grief over a loss or perceived loss.

"No matter how great
the sorrow may be, God
has already suffered it."

— *Meister Eckhart*

# CHAPTER THREE

# IS GRIEVING GOOD FOR YOU?

## *Is The "Grieving Process" Good?*

Even some preachers tell us the so-called grieving process is good. As sincere as they are, it sounds to me like they received their "revelation" from a psychology book, rather than from God's Book. Perhaps they are just using the word "grief" in the wrong context. I don't know. Jesus said, "Blessed are they that mourn." He never said, "Blessed are they that live in grief." In fact, we are told in the book of Isaiah that Jesus, our Lord and Savior, actually bore our griefs and sorrows.

> Surely he [Messiah; Jesus] hath borne our griefs, and carried our sorrows...
>
> — Isaiah 53:4

*19*

When you face a loss, you can do only one of two things. You can go forward or you can go backward. You can become better or you can grow worse. The outcome of your life after facing a loss will depend upon your decisions. If you decide to allow the spirit (or attitude) of grief to stay with you, your life will deteriorate and you will eventually self-destruct. This is what I have seen in over two decades of pastoral ministry.

Elmer (not his real name) chose to stay in a constant state of grief after his 17-year-old son was killed in a road accident. Elmer became bitter. He developed strange patterns, like constantly cutting on his hand with a jack knife. He became a loner and couldn't seem to get along with people. Cynicism and negativity gained a foothold in his life making him miserable to be around. Soon, he had no friends.

One morning I awoke to a phone call. Elmer had committed suicide by taking a shotgun to his chest. The consequences of unresolved grief can be devastating.

Mr. and Mrs. "H" were a happy couple. They had a beautiful, talented child who grew to look like Elvis Presley. They had the "world by the tail," so-to-speak. But Mr. "H" suddenly died. After the funeral, Mrs. "H" started becoming stranger and stranger. After a few months, she nailed sheets over all the windows in her house. She was never seen in the daytime. She'd only come out at night, after dark, when people couldn't see her face. Grief was tormenting her. It was embarrassing and humiliating to her handsome son, but she had made a choice to allow the spirit of grief to cling onto her like a deadly serpent. It was as if her life had just stopped. And that's exactly what the devil wants.

## The Pain Of Saying "Good-bye"

I know the pain of saying "good-bye" to someone you love. It's awful. The pain is real. The lonely Christmases, the empty birthdays, and the weary holidays all serve as gruesome reminders that your loved one is gone. The feelings are real. The emotions are intense. But that doesn't mean these feelings are true or dependable. Feelings and emotions are *not* dependable or accurate most of the time, but God's Word is.

You can rebound, or you can rebel. Mourning can be good, because it will turn to joy.

> ... for I will turn their mourning into joy, and will comfort them, and make them rejoice from their sorrow.
>
> — Jeremiah 31:13b

**21**

Mourning is healthy, because it will turn to dancing (Psalm 30:11). But grief will erode all your passion and put you on the road to rebellion and subsequent destruction. I've seen it over and over again as a pastor.

## The Story of a Real Hero; A Victorious Overcomer

We had a precious 85-year-old church member we affectionately called "Shorty." I received a phone call that Shorty's wife of over 60 years had just died suddenly, so I drove over to Shorty's apartment in the city housing project. There he sat in his little living room with a silly smile on his face. I tried to comfort him by saying, "Shorty, I'm so sorry you lost your precious wife."

"Oh, I didn't lose her," he responded to this young pastor, "I know right where she's at!" It was almost as if he was envious that she went to Heaven first.

Of course, Shorty mourned for his wife. Sure, he missed her. He was lonely for her at times. He had many blessed memories of their life and service for Christ together. But Shorty refused to allow the spirit of grief to rest upon him. He started working around the apartment building, planting flowers, mowing the lawn, and cleaning things for people. He made himself so valuable to the complex, the city leaders lowered his rent because of all the work he was doing around the building. He took on more, blessing all these elderly folks who lived in the building. He'd help the people who locked themselves out of their apartments, arranged Bible studies, and stayed very active. Soon, because he had made himself so valuable to the complex, the city started paying him to live in the apartment. Everybody else's rent was going up, but they were now paying Shorty to live in that complex because he had become so useful and productive.

You see, he mourned, but that mourning turned into dancing and joy because he refused to allow that attitude of grief to penetrate his heart.

I could recount case after case of those who rebounded from a loss. When they rebounded, they became more productive, more successful, and more prosperous than before. Unfortunately, I can also recount cases of those who rebelled by accepting grief as a way of life. They went backwards, and were bitten by the snake of grief and subsequently destroyed. It's a choice.

*"Grief is the agony of
an instant; the indulgence
of grief, the blunder
of a life."*

— *Benjamin Disraeli*

# CHAPTER FOUR

# SYMPTOMS OF THE SPIRIT OF GRIEF

## *Some Signs That The Spirit Or Attitude Of Grief Is Gaining A Foothold*

I have noticed some symptoms which seem to appear in those who have chosen to rebel rather than to rebound. Remember that rebelling comes as a result of allowing grief to retain a strong place in the heart.

1. *Strange patterns begin to develop,* like setting an extra place at the table for the loved one who has gone to Heaven.

2. *A general overall sense of gloom,* sadness, and hopelessness is on the countenance of the person who has chosen to give in to the spirit of grief.

**3.** *A dwindling interest in other people.* I know a pastor who today is in a major state of rebellion and darkness. He is on the scrap heap of life. As a pastor, he had become very politically active. He seemed depressed constantly at the way our nation was going politically and morally. It seemed that all he could focus on was the negative and corrupt. It's all he could talk about. One day, one of his pet "issues" lost a vote at a city council meeting, and this brother went into grief. He lost his interest in preaching and soul winning. He began to develop a careless attitude toward people. Soon, he was drinking alcohol, left the ministry, and his life was destroyed. You see, it was his *perceived* loss that opened the door to the spirit of grief. The fact is, his loss was only a minor issue in the bigger picture, but he saw it as a total defeat.

**4.** *A change in eating or sleeping habits.*

**5.** *The age-old trick of casting blame.*

**6.** *Incessantly talking about the past* rather than the present and the future.

**7.** *Sloppiness and undependability begin showing up.*

**8.** *Irritations become increasingly frequent.*

**9.** *A bitterness of spirit develops and gains a foothold.* In Psalm 73:21(in the Amplified Bible), grieving and bitterness are linked together.

> For my heart was grieved, embittered, and in a
> state of ferment, and I was pricked in my heart
> [as with the sharp fang of an adder].
>
> — **Psalm 73:21 AMPL**

In Hebrews we are told to look "diligently lest any man fail of the grace of God; lest any root of bitterness springing up trouble you, and thereby many be defiled," (Hebrews 12:15). The spirit of grief will lead to bitterness of heart, stop the grace of God from working in your life, and end up defiling you. That's pretty strong.

After I had just accepted the calling as pastor of Mount Hope Church in Lansing, Michigan, I decided to call some of the people on the old rosters to find out what had happened to them. I remember calling a lady whom I'll call Irene.

"Hello, Irene, this is Pastor Williams, the new pastor at Mount Hope Church. I found your name on an old roster and was wondering how you are doing."

"I'm not doing well at all," she snipped back at me.

I asked if we could provide her with transportation to church.

"I haven't been to *that* church in 17 years," she whined, "and I never will come to *that* church or any other church for that matter." I proceeded to ask her what the problem was.

"That song leader offended me 17 years ago, so I left and vowed never to go to church again. Then God took my husband. And now I'm all crippled up with arthritis ... so I couldn't get out of the house even if I wanted to."

Bitterness flowed from her lips like poison for a solid thirty minutes. I tried to comfort and reason with her, and even offered to pray with her, but she rejected my invitation. My mind went to Hebrews 12:15 and I realized how bitterness can trouble people, not only emotionally, but physically as well.

Seventeen years ago, a song leader said something to Irene that caused her to *lose* something; maybe a little pride or a little self-esteem. She then made a decision to cuddle up to the spirit of grief, which turned to bitterness, and ultimately sprung on her like a trap. It bit like a snake.

**10.** *An erosion of spiritual passion sets in.* The things that once excited you have now grown stale and moldy.

**11.** *A desire to run away from all responsibility.*

**12.** *A general loss of self worth.*

I received a call late one night at my home. A lady was sobbing and screaming, "Dave's dead. Dave's dead." A handsome, popular seventeen-year-old high school student named Dave had deliberately ended his life. Why did he do it? Grief.

A series of events had brought this young man into the tormenting cave of grief. He lost his girlfriend; she broke up with him. He was expelled from school for some minor infraction. He had lost his job, and somehow thought he was losing his health. All these "losses" brought a tremendous load of sorrow to the young man and the spirit of grief convinced him that he no longer had any worth to anyone and that life was not worth living.

The spirit of grief is destructive.

We all have suffered pain and loss. But the Bible tells us, as believers, to "sorrow not as others who have no hope" (1 Thessalonians 4:13). Hope is simply a bright picture, or vision of your future.

Sorrow and grief rob you of a bright future.

## The "Valley Of Tears"

Mourning is an outward manifestation of an inner pain. It is not the same as staying in a constant state of grief. Mourning, in a scriptural way will bring blessings, enlargement, and set you in a wealthy place.

> ... we went through fire and through water: but thou broughtest us out into a wealthy place.
>
> — Psalm 66:12b

On our journey through life, we will all face the pain of a personal "Baca." Sooner or later we come to its borders. Many have slipped here and fallen to the spirit of grief.

> How amiable *are* thy tabernacles, O LORD of hosts! My soul longeth, yea, even fainteth for the courts of the LORD: my heart and my flesh crieth out for the living God. Yea, the sparrow hath found an house, and the swallow a nest for

herself, where she may lay her young, *even* thine altars, O LORD of hosts, my King, and my God. Blessed *are* they that dwell in thy house: they will be still praising thee. Selah. Blessed *is* the man whose strength *is* in thee; in whose heart *are* the ways *of them. Who* passing through the valley of Baca make it a well; the rain also filleth the pools. They go from strength to strength, *every one of them* in Zion appeareth before God.

— Psalm 84:1-7

The Valley of Baca in Psalm 84:1-7 was an actual place known as the "Valley of Tears" or the "Valley of Weeping." It has come to symbolize any tough or painful event that causes us to hurt emotionally. It's a place of seeming uncertainty and stress. But, God made rock-solid promises for those who would go *through* the Valley of Baca and resolve *not* to stop there. He promised that Baca would only be a *temporary point* in your journey through life. He promised that you would be filled with an unlimited supply (rain for your pools), and that you would gain a supernatural victorious power! All this is promised to those who mourn, but refuse to slip into the attitude of grief.

*"There is a sweet joy
that comes to us through
sorrow."*

— *Charles H. Spurgeon*

# CHAPTER FIVE

# THE ROAD TO RECOVERY

I know you want to go forward and not backward. You want to become better, not bitter. You want to rebound, not rebel. Then allow me to present you with seven simple keys for the kind of mourning that leads to joy, dancing, and increase.

*Number 1 — Set a time limit for your mourning.* You have heard the expression "Time heals all wounds." Don't believe it. Time doesn't heal anything. Five years after my dad died, I still was not healed from that trauma that took place back in 1966. Waiting around for time to heal your pain is fruitless. Jesus is the healer.

I read about a precious man who received a nightmarish call one night that his entire family was killed in a school bus that was hit by a drunk driver. His wife of 18 years and his two beautiful teen-age daughters were gone. Time did not heal his pain as he rehearsed in his mind how his loved ones burned to death in that fiery crash. He could find no real peace or relief from the pain until he made the decision to set a time limit on his mourning. He set a date for it to be over, after which he would refuse to mourn. When he did this, God worked a miracle in his heart and restored his passion, gave him another beautiful wife and a new start in life. You must set a time limit on mourning if it is to turn to joy and dancing.

*Number 2 — Pray in the Spirit.* Proverbs 3:5 tells us to "lean not unto our own understanding." Often when the spirit of grief strikes, you'll hear people say, "I just don't understand . . .." But when we pray in the spirit, we pray without our human understanding (1 Corinthians 14:2, 14, 15). During these seasons of prayer, God just may reveal wonderful things to you about your loved one. He may show you important keys and principles to apply in your life. Your own spirit will be energized, built up (1 Corinthians 14:4, Jude 20), and you will gain heavenly understanding.

*Number 3 — Ask the Lord to give your loved one a message.* Necromancy is forbidden in the Bible. This is the practice of talking to the dead. Prayer to God, however, is not forbidden, but encouraged. I remember standing at my father's gravestone fourteen years after he had died. It was the first time I ever visited his grave. I stood there weeping, thinking of all the things I wished I had said to my dad when he was alive. Then I remembered looking up into the heavens and saying, "Jesus, You are God. Will you please tell my dad that I love him — I really love him? And let him know that I'm a preacher now, if he doesn't already know. Tell him he'd be proud of me, like he was when I'd win the track meets back in high school. Thank you, Lord." What a peace enveloped me. What an amazing release. Something happened that closed the book on all those guilt-ridden years of never telling my dad that I loved him.

*Number 4 — Start praising God with reckless abandon.* Lift your hands. Dance around your house shouting praises to God and watch how the garment of praise peels off that old rag of heaviness.

> ... to comfort all that mourn; to appoint unto them that mourn in Zion, to give unto them beauty for ashes, the oil of joy for mourning, the garment of praise for the spirit of heaviness; that they might be called trees of righteousness, the planting of the Lord, that He might be glorified.
>
> — Isaiah 61:2b-3

*Number 5 — Speak out loud to others of your intention to move ahead in God's will, regardless of this setback.* You see, the devil can make some pretty powerful arguments for your right to grieve. He will accuse you, tell you all the wrong things you said or did, and use any other tool he can employ to get you into a position of perpetual grief. Only faith-filled words spoken from God's revealed will can neutralize him and drive his thoughts far from your mind. Jesus used simple phrases from God's Word to overcome the devil. Speak God's Word, God's will, and your intentions of moving ahead.

I was honored to have a part in Gabrielle Christian Salem's memorial service in Tulsa, Oklahoma in November of 1999. It was an emotionally and spiritually moving time. Many people had wonderful words to say about this precious six-year old daughter of Harry and Cheryl Salem. I had only known "Gab" for a couple of years, but I really loved her. She was small, but, oh what an undeniable anointing she carried. There were so many touching things about her little life.

The speakers and singers at her memorial service were anointed and powerful. Yet the most powerful part of the entire service was when her parents Harry and Cheryl, came to the platform and affirmed their faith in God, and the fact that they were going to move ahead with God, in spite of this confusing situation that nobody seemed to understand.

*Number 6 — Get busy again.* Do whatever it is you are called to do. It's okay to take a short break, but there comes a time to get up and move on.

When Elijah started grieving because revival had not come to Israel and Jezebel wanted his head on a platter, he ran away, stopped under a juniper tree and just stayed there. But there came a time when God sent him the clear message, "It's time to move on now. You're a prophet, it's time to start prophesying again."

Start moving ahead, and verbalize to as many people as possible your full intentions of serving God all the days of your life, no matter what. It will not only help bring you into a "wealthy place," (Psalm 66:12) it will be a witness to others of your abiding faith in Jesus Christ. Those who allow their lives to stop because of the spirit of grief can never be a witness of Christ's amazing love and restoring power.

*Number 7 — Give Jesus Christ your life, if you haven't already.* Only He has the power to make all things new. God gave only one plan to make you fit for Heaven, and that plan is a Man – Jesus Christ. It was He who took our infirmities and bore our sicknesses. He bore our griefs and sorrows, and He alone has the power to pull you through the "Valley of Tears" successfully. God has no "Plan B."

Jesus was God incarnate. He died on the cross and rose from the dead. It is Jesus who sent the Holy Spirit, the Divine Comforter. If you've never received Jesus Christ, do it right now.

> But as many as received him, to them gave he the power to become the sons of God, even to them that believe on his name.
>
> — John 1:12

Simply tell God, wherever you are right now, that you have sinned and fallen short of His standards.

> For all have sinned, and come short of the glory of God.
>
> — Romans 3:23

Ask Jesus to be your Savior and only hope. Then say, "Jesus, You are my Lord." Tell someone you prayed and that Jesus Christ is now your Lord, and that you have been given a brand new start in life.

> That if thou shalt confess with thy mouth the Lord Jesus, and shalt believe in thine heart that God raised him from the dead, thou shalt be saved. For with the heart man believeth unto righteousness and with the mouth confession is made unto salvation.
>
> — Romans 10:9, 10

> Therefore if any man be in Christ, he is a new creature: old things are passed away; behold, all things become new.
>
> — 2 Corinthians 5:17

This is the starting point for turning mourning into joy and dancing. God is crazy in love with you. If you haven't done it already, accept His love as a free gift.

> For God so loved the world, that he gave his only begotten Son, that whosoever believeth in him should not perish, but have everlasting life. For God sent not his Son into the world to condemn the world; but that the world through him might be saved.
>
> — John 3:16, 17

When you receive Jesus Christ, you can then ask Him to send you the Divine Comforter; the Holy Spirit. Then your mourning will turn to overflowing joy. Look what Jesus said about this:

> And I will pray the Father, and he shall give you another Comforter, that he may abide with you for ever; even the Spirit of Truth ...
>
> — John 14:16, 17a

> He that believeth on me, as the scriptures hath said, out of his belly shall flow rivers of living water. (But this spake he of the Spirit, which they that believe on him should receive ...)
>
> — John 8:38, 39a

## The Choice is Yours

Rebel or rebound? The choice belongs to each of us. We can go forward with our lives or we can go backwards. I know you are choosing to rebound, like Harry and Cheryl Salem have. Just wait. You will see a bright, abundant future begin to unfold before your very eyes. Watch for it, beginning RIGHT NOW!

## *From Mourning To Morning*

For a more complete study on the subject of mourning and grief, I strongly suggest that you get a copy of Harry & Cheryl Salem's book, *From Mourning To Morning*. You may write or call Harry and Cheryl Salem at:

Harry and Cheryl Salem
PO Box 701287
Tulsa, OK 74170
(918) 298-0770

or visit their web site at:
www.salemfamilyministries.org

# About The Author

Dave Williams is pastor of Mount Hope Church and International Outreach Ministries, with world headquarters in Lansing, Michigan. He has served for 20 years, leading the church in Lansing from 226 to over 4000 today. Dave sends trained ministers into unreached cities to establish disciple-making churches, and, as a result, today has "branch" churches in the United States, Philippine Islands, and in Africa.

Dave is the founder and president of Mount Hope Bible Training Institute, a fully accredited institute for training ministers and lay people for the work of the ministry. He has authored 39 books including the fifteen-time best seller, The Start of Something Wonderful (with over 2,000,000 books sold), and more recently, The Miracle Results of Fasting.

The Pacesetter's Path telecast is Dave's weekly television program seen over a syndicated network of secular stations. Dave has produced over 90 audio cassette programs including the nationally acclaimed School of Pacesetting Leadership which is being used as a training program in churches around the United States, and in Bible schools in South Africa and the Philippines. He is a popular speaker at conferences, seminars, and conventions. His speaking ministry has taken him across America, Africa, Europe, Asia, and other parts of the world.

Along with his wife, Mary Jo, Dave established The Dave and Mary Jo Williams Charitable Mission (Strategic Global Mission), a missions ministry for providing scholarships to pioneer pastors, and grants to inner-city children's ministries.

Dave's articles and reviews have appeared in national magazines such as Advance, The Pentecostal Evangel, Ministries Today, The Lansing Magazine, The Detroit Free Press and others. Dave, as a private pilot, flies for fun. He is married, has two children, and lives in Delta Township, Michigan.

*You may write to Pastor Dave Williams:*

> *P.O. Box 80825*
> *Lansing, MI 48908-0825*

*Please include your special prayer requests when you write, or you may call the Mount Hope Global Prayer Center anytime:*
> *1-517-327-PRAY*

**Published by**

# DECAPOLIS
# PUBLISHING

*For a catalog of products, call:*

*1-517-321-2780 or*

*1-800-888-7284*

*or visit us on the web at:*

*www.mounthopechurch.org*

## *Mount Hope Ministries*

Mount Hope Missions & International Outreach
Care Ministries, Deaf Ministries & Support Groups
Access to Christ for the Physically Impaired
Community Outreach Ministries
Mount Hope Youth Ministries
Mount Hope Bible Training Institute
The Hope Store and Decapolis Publishing
The Pacesetter's Path Telecast
The Pastor's Minute Radio Broadcast
Mount Hope Children's Ministry
Sidewalk Sunday School
The Saturday Care Clinic

When you're facing a struggle and need someone
to pray with you, please call us at (517) 321-CARE
or (517) 327-PRAY. We have pastors on duty 24
hours a day. We know you hurt sometimes and
need a pastor, a minister, or a prayer partner. There
will be ministers and prayer partners here for you.

If you'd like to write, we'd be honored to pray for
you. Our address is: *MOUNT HOPE CHURCH*
*202 S. CREYTS RD. LANSING, MI 48917*
**(517) 321-CARE • (517) 321-2780**
**(517) 327-PRAY**

*www.mounthopechurch.org*
*www.christian.tv/*
*dave_williams.phtml*
*mhc@mounthopechurch.org*

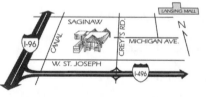

West of the Lansing Mall, on Creyts at Michigan Ave.

# For Your Spiritual Growth

Here's the help you need for your spiritual journey. These books will encourage you, and give you guidance as you seek to draw close to Jesus and learn of Him. Prepare yourself for fantastic growth!

**SOMEBODY OUT THERE NEEDS YOU**
*Along with the gift of salvation comes the great privilege of spreading the gospel of Jesus Christ.*

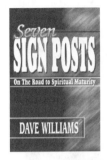

**SEVEN SIGNPOSTS TO SPIRITUAL MATURITY**
*Examine your life to see where you are on the road to spiritual maturity.*

**THE PASTORS PAY**
*How much is your pastor worth? Who should set his pay? Discover the scriptural guidelines for paying your pastor.*

**DECEPTION, DELUSION & DESTRUCTION**
*Recognize spiritual deception and unmask spiritual blindness.*

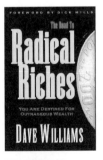

**THE ROAD TO RADICAL RICHES**
*Are you ready to jump from "barely getting by" to Gods plan for putting you on the road to Radical Riches?*

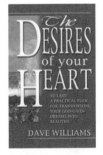

**THE DESIRES OF YOUR HEART**
*Yes, Jesus wants to give you the desires of your heart, and make them realities.*

These and other books
available from Dave Williams and:

DECAPOLIS PUBLISHING

# For Your Spiritual Growth

Here's the help you need for your spiritual journey. These books will encourage you, and give you guidance as you seek to draw close to Jesus and learn of Him. Prepare yourself for fantastic growth!

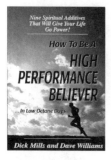

**HOW TO BE A HIGH PERFORMANCE BELIEVER**
*Pour in the nine spiritual additives for real power in your Christian life.*

**SECRET OF POWER WITH GOD**
*Tap into the real power with God; the power of prayer. It will change your life!*

**THE NEW LIFE ... THE START OF SOMETHING WONDERFUL**
*You can get off to a great start on your exciting new life with Jesus! Prepare for something wonderful.*

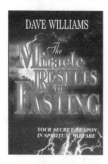

**MIRACLE RESULTS OF FASTING**
*You can receive MIRACLE benefits, spiritually and physically, with this practical Christian discipline.*

**WHAT TO DO IF YOU MISS THE RAPTURE**
*If you miss the Rapture, there may still be hope, but you need to follow these clear survival tactics.*

**THE AIDS PLAGUE**
*Is there hope? Yes, but only Jesus can bring a total and lasting cure to AIDS.*

# For Your Spiritual Growth

Here's the help you need for your spiritual journey. These books will encourage you, and give you guidance as you seek to draw close to Jesus and learn of Him. Prepare yourself for fantastic growth!

**THE ART OF PACESETTING LEADERSHIP**
*You can become a successful leader with this proven leadership development course.*

**GIFTS THAT SHAPE YOUR LIFE**
*Learn which ministry best fits you, and discover your God-given personality gifts, as well as the gifts of others.*

**GROWING UP IN OUR FATHER'S FAMILY**
*You can have a family relationship with your heavenly father. Learn how God cares for you.*

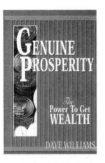

**SUPERNATURAL SOULWINNING**
*How will we reach our family, friends, and neighbors in this short time before Christ's return?*

**THE GRAND FINALE**
*What will happen in the days ahead just before Jesus' return? Will you be ready for the grand finale?*

**GENUINE PROSPERITY**
*Learn what it means to be truly prosperous! God gives us the power to get wealth!*

**These and other books available from Dave Williams and:**

DECAPOLIS
PUBLISHING

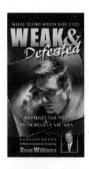